Police Academy Training

Survival Tips from a Veteran Academy Instructor

By

Brad Anderson

TABLE OF CONTENTS

ABOUT THE AUTHOR

I appreciate you taking time to read this book, thank you. I have been where you are, and I was worried about how I would take on the daunting task of completing the police academy. My friends and family were all watching but, more than that, so were the officers that I would be working with. I applied this information I am about to share with you to myself as I endured my own academy experience.

Years after graduating, and receiving the "Top Cop Award", which is also known as graduating first in my class, this information is as relevant as ever. I was able to craft this information into a useful guide for you to use in your own journey.

Currently, I am a law enforcement academy instructor at a recognized and accredited academy, and I train heroes for a living. I have seen many successful cadets as well as a lot of failed attempts due to poor planning and preparation. I will do

my best to share the highlights of what you need to know to be

one of the success stories.

PREFACE

I'd like to start with a little mental exercise. Think of a police officer, one that's perfect in your mind. What do they look like? Do they appear confident in a well-tailored uniform, polished brass, and shined boots? Are they athletically built? Are they well-spoken and knowledgeable of the law? Are they someone you could trust?

The truth is, before they ever became that glorious picture of perfection in your mind… they had to survive me. It's my job to create what you see. I'm their police academy instructor.

I, and many like me, bear the responsibility of sending these men and women into harm's way, and we take it very seriously. It's not like learning any other skill or trade. Usually, if you have a bad day at your job, the penalty is manageable. If these moms and dads, sons and daughters, but most of all, people, have a bad day, they might not make it home. The price they pay is staggeringly high.

I think every kid probably wanted to be a cop at some point growing up, at least I did. Not so sure if this is what I pictured though. Now a days, we've become targets of hatred and violence, not to everyone, but a lot of people. That gets to be tough, mentally, on an officer over the years.

That's only part of it. Because, anyone that can do shift work or nights for 20 years is my hero, and good luck having a healthy home life. But still, there is so much more negative about this job. Sometimes it seems to outweigh the positives.

Now with that being said, you have a small idea of what I have to prepare these men and women for. The capacity of the individuals that can handle everything it takes to be a public servant is rough. They are truly a select breed.

I'm going to take you into this world, from day one. We will explore what you need to know about graduating a police academy. It won't be easy…no, really, it's supposed to be hard. We have to determine who has the potential of being that picture in your mind from those who just want a badge. Some language may be offensive, but so are the real streets in America. If a bad word or two offends you, this profession may not be right for you. It requires you to be thick skinned sometimes.

I've already enjoyed visiting with you about this, and I hope to see you on graduation day if this is what you choose. But before then, we've got work to do. So for all of you that may have just arrived at my academy, get ready for the screaming, or as I like to call it, my VERY LOUD TONE.

INTRODUCTION

My name is Instructor, I build heroes for a living, and this is my house. I am not your friend, nor your enemy, and to be honest, I'm not interested in your sensitivity issues one way or the other. If you have these issues, then you made a wrong turn when you showed up at my house, and I have a job to do at my house. I build tools that people can't live without, regardless of what they may believe. I own the responsibility of turning the average man or woman into something different, or unique.

The people that I train are the ones that run at trouble when everyone else is running from it. They will look the devil in his eyes as they formulate a plan to defeat him. They have a belief that they are the thin blue line between what is good in this world and what the scariest evils that you can imagine are. They will all die for what they believe, just ask them. They are the tools that I have built, and now are my brothers and sisters. I'm so damn proud of them, I can barely stand it.

This book is not for everyone. It is offensive, at best, to anyone not interested in a life of civil servanthood. So, if you think you will glide through my house without your best, and I mean your best…like I said, you took a wrong turn. This is a career that is rewarding to the point of tears and is painful and terrifying as well. I'm also not a writer or an author for a living. So if you believe that certain things are "grammatically incorrect", I didn't write this to satisfy you anyway. This is for the studs and stallions, not the grammar teacher. The minimal editing of this content is intentional, by my request. I need you to be able to understand what I'm saying, really get it. When you show up to my house for training, or my brother's house anywhere in this world, we really don't care if we punctuate good enough for you. By the way, I have arrested a few grammar teachers in my career. I've also arrested a few CEO's. You see, my authority doesn't rest at feet of your money, your color, or anything that you may be in charge of. I build tools that will go to any environment or condition, and perform to the letter of the law. They're also the tools that give up their jacket in the rain to a stranded motorist, or buy a meal for a hungry family that doesn't have much more than they do.

You need to be real sure about this before you step off into my world. You will never be the same, after a certain point. Ask any of my brothers and sisters. Doing this job is like the air in our lungs. There's no half-assing in this game. People really die.

BEFORE YOU SHOW UP

Ok then, since you're still reading, let's talk about some details that are vital for survival in my house. You also should assume, as your reading this, that I am giving you this information in a VERY LOUD TONE, constantly! I am not a doctor, nor do I play one on TV. But, you need to know if you have any physical limitations before you arrive. Your hiring department should have you complete a medical exam. Most academies will not allow you to participate without clearance from a medical professional. A commitment to health is essential for mind and body. It is one of the pieces that helps a person deal with the stress and adaptive circumstances of this profession.

Most people do not realize that in order to inspire change, you have to be focused in everything you do, including a schedule. The biggest shock to a cadet can be the simplest things that no one ever thinks about. For example, I have never seen a police academy operated where the recruits or cadets have a refrigerator available to them or snack time. Acclimate yourself to a three-meal-a-day diet. You would not believe how many people think that they are starving, and drop out early, because of terrible food habits prior to arrival. If you can't control what you eat and the portions now, how do you expect to make the adjustment when you don't have a choice?

Next, your physical conditioning needs to be the priority in your life. A good cardio and strength building schedule should be implemented long before day one of the academy. I get a lot of questions from people about what the requirements are. I have two responses.

1) Every academy has strict regulations, in reference to graduation requirements, for physical training. They also have a percentage that will allow people to participate. This is not the same as the percentage to graduate. In other words, you may make it in to the academy, at 60 percent physically, but to graduate and pass the P.T. test,

you may need to be at 90 percent or higher. Along with this is a consideration of age and gender as well. Do your due diligence and know what your state requirements are, based on your particular information. It is typically on a state's website or can be given to you by your department's training officer. This can be a valuable tool. If I were you, and I was worried about my conditioning, I would take the requirements to a fitness coach or a local gym. These people make a living turning average people into athletes. They can design a plan that is tailored to your body type, and even help with meal planning. If this is a troubling area for you, then invest in yourself, and get a coach. Also, investing in a high quality pair of running shoes is very important.

2) This response is what I was told by my academy P.T. instructor, in a VERY LOUD TONE: "If someone just shot your partner, and your weapon would not fire, and you had to chase em' for three miles, and then he

wanted to fight you to the death.......Are you gonna tell your partner's wife and children that you didn't have what it took to finish the fight?" Simmer on that one for a minute.

DAY ONE'S WELCOMING COMMITTEE

You are not fit mentally, you are not fit physically, you can't do anything correctly, you are not on time by "my watch", and you sure as hell suck at managing yourself! Expect all of this to be true and much, much more! I will be more than happy to remind you of all these things in a, VERY LOUD TONE, constantly! Every recruit or cadet seems to think that this is a very difficult day. Well guess what, it is, and it's supposed to suck! My fellow instructors and I don't believe that you are here for the right reasons, and until you show us different, we will treat you as such. Usually, I can expect 15% out of the people you showed up with to be gone in about 90 minutes. Let the quitters leave my house, better now than when you need them.

Here are a few things you can expect. There will be a lot of yelling, from everybody. There will also be a lot of exercising and running. I affectionately call this motivation and corrective measures, but you will see it as punishment. I am not punishing you! What you don't realize is that I am already evaluating you. The reason you need to have a good fitness level when you arrive is because you are immediately undergoing stress training.

If I asked you to do 10 pushups, you could. But, if I TOLD you to do 10 pushups, in a VERY LOUD TONE, while telling you to count them, yelling all around you, and before I let you up, you have to tell me what you learned, you may not be able to do 5 pushups.

Stress is very different when you are in battle. It can affect you in many ways, one of those ways is physically. You will feel fatigued 40 percent faster than normal. What that means is, you're going to feel tired really fast. Even if you know that your body is used to doing much more than this, it won't matter. The difference is stress. I will teach you to manage it.

Next thing, unless you are prior military, you are expected to do a lot of new things incorrectly. We know that before you arrive. That is why there are so many of us available for yelling and offering you corrective measures. Someone may need an additional level of support, so we have the people that can work with them without holding back the rest of the group. Do not let the amount of instructors stress you out. Also, we will never lie to you. So if you are instructed to run and get your gear, then that is exactly what I meant. I would not recommend walking if I told you to run.

This brings me to one of the most important points of day one. Learn to listen, very carefully, to the instructions that you are given. This screws up more people than anything, seriously. Someone, inevitably, will do what they think is better or what they think they heard. This will cause a lot of corrective measures. And, since you are part of a developing team, you will probably be corrected together, a lot. I only did 10 pushups myself the first day of my academy due to some corrective measures. But, I did a whole lot more than that with my class by the end of the day.

Let me help you have a little comfort here. Everyone that's yelling at you is trained to do so. What you see as chaos is actually more like a perfect symphony to us. We know how much to push, we know how much to yell, and we know how much you can take mentally and physically, even if you don't. Remember, we build tools. If you could transform yourself alone, you wouldn't be here, we will help you. However, if we see someone that is lagging behind or not giving all they have in any area, we are drawn to it like sharks in bloody water. Stress will make you want to take short cuts, and short cuts equal corrective measures and eviction from my house.

Next thing, let's talk about attitude. I have a very high expectation in reference to yours. I can help you learn the basics and teach you how to march, but I can't teach you manners. I will never allow you to be disrespectful to one of my instructors, myself, or your new team. It is the quickest way to get thrown out of my house. I will also be calling your Chief or Supervisor to tell him about your actions. That typically will end very badly for you. Teaching you how to manage stress is very different than helping you with your attitude. I expect you to come to my house with a mind ready to learn, and a good attitude to go with it. I will not ask you for advice because I am already what you want to be, so keep your mouth shut. This environment is necessary for you. Its purpose is to help you take in maximum information in minimal time. You wouldn't be wise to interrupt a dispatcher that is giving you a description of a murder suspect around the corner from where you are patrolling, so don't interrupt the instructors. We have a purpose for everything we do. Remember, it's our symphony.

Psychologically, your mind will be in overload for the first few days. This will get better as you begin to figure out the structure of the environment. You will be asking yourself if this was a good idea. Don't worry, that's normal. You will have told yourself a hundred times that you will not quit. Yet, that will be exactly what's on your mind. That's normal too. In fact, I have heard pretty much every recruit's excuse to quit in this house. I'll say this, anyone that wears that badge probably earned it, so I won't be breaking tradition because of you. Quit now and get out of my house, or suck it up. Your department sent you to me because they know I will build them the best officer possible. I don't need someone "covering my six" that can't stand a little yelling, or gets their feeling hurt so easily. Your training environment is controlled, the streets you patrol are not. When you lose control of yourself, physically or emotionally, you become distracted. Distractions can be deadly.

Do yourself a favor and relax. All you have to do is what you're told, and help your new brothers and sisters. Do that well, and things become tolerable. You may never have another chance to learn without the distractions that life can bring. You might as well make the best of it. You will be nervous, shaking, confused because of stress, and exhausted.

You will probably feel all of this within a few minutes of arrival. Once again, all normal. Stress tolerance is like a muscle, use it and it gets stronger and stronger. You will become more and more adapted to the environment of stress, and it won't take long to improve. You will be able to overcome things in your mind that you have previously seen as barriers. This is our symphony, and we do it well.

Last, but certainly not least, is to be well hydrated for day one. Have you ever seen someone stressed out that's sweating a lot? That will be you. Add corrective measures and stress, you will be cramping up in no time. I am personally not a fan of pain. I will push through it, if I have to. But, if I can avoid pain by proper planning, I will happily do that instead. If you cramp up in the middle of corrective measures that I gave to you, I still expect completion of my corrective measures. If you are not well hydrated for at least a week in advance, then you have planned poorly, and you will pay, painfully, with cramping and poor performance.

We do not reward or wait for those who have planned poorly. You knew, going into this, that some planning was necessary. So, if you show up after having a breakfast buffet, you're physically a fat body, haven't been drinking lots of water a day for the previous week, and don't have your mind right, you just showed up to my house woefully unprepared. You will probably be gone very quickly. It's not difficult if you're totally prepared. This is really all you need to make it through day one.

Let us talk about friends and family. Yes they love you, yes they will miss you, and yes, they may want to celebrate before you leave or on your time off. Remember, alcohol dehydrates your body. So if you pass out or cramp up during physical training, you have no excuse. I will remind you of your failure in a VERY LOUD TONE.

TEAM LIVING, ROUTINE,

AND INSPECTIONS

At this point, you have survived some of the initial "culling out" of those that didn't want to be here. By the end of the first day, you will have taken in lots of critical information and rules for my house, in a VERY LOUD TONE. Your living arrangements may be barracks, squad rooms, two person rooms, etc. I will share some important details with you that will keep you on track.

First, we do all things together. So, if I show your roommate how I expect their locker or closet to be set up, yours should be identical, and I do mean identical. Unification is very important in my house. The amount of detail that I expect you to adhere to has a huge purpose here that you will learn. I will remind you and your classmates of this in a VERY LOUD TONE often. You will operate as a team, all the same, no color, no gender, and no differences, without exceptions.

There is no place for someone that does not have the discipline to conform to these standards. You have to be vigilant in helping your fellow classmates in this unification process. If you know how to shine boots well, and that's important in my house, shouldn't you share that if someone is struggling? My regular inspection of your living quarters and your dress attire will be brutally strict. Make it easy on yourself and help each other. You won't make graduation if you don't.

The instructors will be looking for things that are random, like a button unfastened on a shirt, in the closet, or pants all hanging in the same direction, personal items that are all in a particular location and the same. Remember, it's in the details, being exact and the same. You will clean better than you have ever cleaned before. I will check for dust on the window seal, over the door, under the bed and furniture, and anywhere else I like. So remember that clean means clean well.

A lot of people struggle with making their bunks. Some instructors will want to see a 4 inch fold, 6 inch or completely mended at the top. We will show you how, and it is inspected daily. Several people have asked me if different instructors look for different things, and the answer is yes. But, it will not be something that you haven't been shown, or is new to you. It will still be unified regardless of the instructor. For example, one instructor will not expect a 6 inch fold on your bed while other instructors expect 4 inches. The instructors will be unified in all expectations.

If you see a classmate being told something in a VERY LOUD TONE, pay attention to the details that they are being corrected for. If this happens to the same classmate multiple times, I will make the entire class pay by corrective measures for not caring enough about the success of each other. I have zero tolerance for someone not willing to give of themselves to help their fellow man. You picked the wrong profession if you are selfish.

Leaders will begin to emerge in this process. They are always people that care about others, and the overall performance of the class. At some point, leadership will be established within the class. This will become the chain of command for the function of the team. They have their own responsibilities, just like others, but have additional tasks given to them based on the willingness to be helpful or motivating.

Once you figure out the routine, and the day to day operations in my house, things become much easier for you. With the small stuff out of the way, and improving daily, the instructors are free to move on to more pressing issues. But, we never go backwards. Once you have learned something, we expected it always. I will smoke your ass in a VERY LOUD TONE for a poorly worn uniform in the first week just as I will the week you graduate.

So we are clear, I can be in a good mood and operate in a VERY LOUD TONE. If I have to "smoke your ass" in a VERY LOUD TONE, it means that the work you are putting forth is embarrassing to me and offensive to those that have come before you. It's the worst of my VERY LOUD TONE and the most serious corrective measures applied.

In fact, I expect better every day, since you are doing it every day. Insiders tip: Don't let me catch your back pocket unbuttoned on your uniform trouser pants, it's my pet peeve. That includes if it's in your closet. Remember, it's all in the details. If we can teach you to be mindful of the details, you will always look your best, write the best reports, and have a willingness to help your fellow man. Everything we do has a bigger picture, and every detail has a reason behind it. Without going into detail, because you should be taught this information by your academy, there are documented cases of officers that were killed because their appearance was sloppy and unprofessional.

At this point, you will begin to settle down a little bit. It will still be stressful, but you will start to respond as a team with action, not panic, not as a single individual. The mindset that you're starting to develop from this process is key for your learning to continue. It also makes things like marching, facing movements, even getting to chow, much easier. You are learning to take action together.

OFF-DUTY CONDUCT

It never fails. Someone is going to do something stupid, on their off time, and get kicked out. I have seen this happen from day one to hours before graduation. What a huge failure and disappointment. Apparently, there exist people who believe we won't find out about poor decisions made while off-duty. The shear nature of doing something that makes you ineligible to continue, after all you are learning at my house, makes me not want you in this profession, ever.

If you have friends that can't understand how important this lifestyle is to you, then I recommend getting some new friends. It's hard to have respect in a community, as a law enforcer, if you're part of the problem on the weekends. You are on the verge of becoming a part of something that is very special. Not only will poor decisions stop you, but could result in you never being allowed in this occupation again.

Let me offer you some things to consider. Officers that have come before you are not your family, yet. If you are caught doing something stupid, I will know about it, because officers will call me first. The next call is to your agency head.

I know what it's like to want to blow off some steam after a stressful week of training, but, the bar scene is a terrible idea. Cadets and recruits get a little liquid courage and nobody likes a-wanna-be rookie running his or her mouth about a hard week. DUI's and fighting are some of the more popular reasons to be kicked out of my house.

Everyone knows how to behave, but I expect way more of you. That's why common sense is so important. The worst one of all, in my humble opinion, is when a recruit or a cadet has law enforcement called on them for their discretionary failure. If you think that real officers will be understanding once they arrive, you are terrible mistaken. They are going to be really pissed off at you! You are the one that may protect their family someday, so that will be very disappointing to them. Getting arrested is about as bad as it gets. They will not help you, because they are better than you at this point, and they had to prove it, like you should be doing. However, your actions will have already told a different story. Again, I am the one that they call, at 2:30 a.m., on my weekend off, from a dead sleep..... Not good for you at all.

I will see you, briefly, Monday morning. It doesn't take long for you to get your gear out of my house.

One of the benefits of being a part of a team, during the week, is that everyone helps everyone else. If you don't hear the alarm because you studied late, your team will cover you, and wake you up. That's what we do. But what about your first day back from your weekend off? What if you're late or don't have your proper equipment? Well that's an easy one. I will make you and your class pay in a, VERY LOUD TONE, with corrective measures until I get tired of watching you strain.

Don't forget what you learn here. It doesn't change when you're on your time. Let's open our minds and look a bit deeper at something. Why do officers call me when a recruit or cadet is in trouble? They call me because I build tools that THEY can count on in the future, forging what could be their partner in the future, tools that protect their family's future. What would you do? They know that the first person that you have failed, outside of yourself, is me. I don't like to fail, or produce failing tools that can't do the job. What do YOU do with broken tools?

PHYSICAL TRAINING (PT), SELF-DEFENSE, AND TESTING

Without a doubt, this course of instruction fails more than half would-be officers than all other reasons combined. Every construction process starts with a strong foundation. Your body is the temple. All things start with a strong mind and body. I said earlier that I recommend a high quality running shoe. One of my graduating classmates took it a step further. He actually went to an athletic shoe store, and let a run professional help him choose a shoe based on his stride, step and a few other things. It was totally worth it if you ask him, as he did win the PT award in my class.

Even people that are relatively fit when they arrive at the academy are prone to common injuries, and the instructors know this. The problem is dumb courage. There are some that will keep PT injuries quiet, and while I admire your attempt to be strong and fight through the pain, it's not worth permanent damage in the future. It happens in self-defense training also.

There may be a time in your career where you have to fight

through a disabling injury, but it's not while you are in my

care. I expect you to be honest about any injuries that you may

acquire during training.

With that being said, I will smoke your ass in a VERY

LOUD TONE if you sandbag on me. A sand bagger is

someone who doesn't believe they have to give all they have in

training. The instructors know the difference between injuries

and laziness. The PT instructors and the self-defense

instructors are not only instructors, but they are required to

regularly train and carry additional certificates to teach these

courses. The only thing sandbagging gets you is more reasons

to have more corrective measures, for you and your team.

There are a few simple things you can do to help with

recovery and overall health while you're in the academy. One

is hygiene. There is a lot of sweating, fighting, running, and

much more. Staying clean keeps the chances of a staph

infection low. It's also not fun when you're wrestling with a guy that smells like garbage.

Because some of you will be pushing new levels in physical fitness, pay attention to your feet. Athlete's foot affects men and women, and can be really painful and gross if not tended to. When you are sweating in those shoes for several hours, problems can happen. I recommend a spray for your shoes. That helps prevent problems from starting. At my academy, I do not allow medications unless prescribed, and approved, in advance. If you need a basic pain reliever, that's acceptable, but I want to know about it and why. It's my job to take care of my tools like it's your job to take care of your body.

When you are learning defensive tactics, strains and pulled muscles are common. Athletic tape is beneficial if approved by your instructors. What both of these courses have in common is that they require physical exertion. You are going to be sore, so expect it. Have a mental plan to deal with it. Also, at my academy, both of these courses are pass or fail. Work hard so you can exceed the minimal expectations and shine as a leader.

Testing in these courses is easy, if you prepared properly. You should already know what you need for PT testing success before you arrive, we talked about this earlier. If you are short on your pushup count, you should be doing pushups every chance you get. If you have a problem with a technique for self-defense, one of your classmates should be willing to help you work through it. Focus on your needs, and help others where they are weak. Remember, we leave no one behind.

SOCIAL MEDIA AND IMAGES

If you like being a social media mega star, this part is for you. If you think that people are not influenced by the things you're posting, you're wrong. Social media can be the devil if you're not careful. Nothing like seeing a picture of a cadet in his uniform, bold and strong, right next to a picture of him drunk and passed out at the club.

This has not always been an issue, but in recent years, more and more officers are being fired from law enforcement, and the academy because of their posts, videos, and pictures. If good people are on social media, that means bad people, and drama queens are too. If I catch you on social media referring to, or showing a video of the tactics you are learning, you are causing a threat to the law enforcement community, and I will put you out of my house immediately.

Also, use some common sense, and have some respect for yourself. If you take a picture of the person that you are becoming, don't tarnish it by other crap on your pages. This is a real issue. Bad guys use the information on your profile to gain intelligence. They know your age, who you hang out with, and where you frequent. Social media is as beneficial as a phonebook, and everyone knows it. If you don't have the common sense to know what will and will not potentially hurt your reputation, then just get rid of it.

If you can't live without your social media, do what you want, but I would not say a word about what I do for a living. And remember, sometimes it is not what you post, it's what overly dramatic people find to rant about. Remember, everybody loves a cop until one pisses them off. Leave no "ammo" behind to be used against you.

FIREARMS TRAINING

Firearms training is an essential skill that every cadet needs to master. While I hope you never have to use this particular skill set, I expect you to be surgical if you do. You will learn that shooting a weapon is much more than just pulling a trigger. You will be tasked with performing at a much higher level than any civilian you will ever encounter. You will have to account for every shot that is on target, and every shot that misses in the real world. This can be challenging for beginners. Some recruits have never held or fired a weapon before. It has been my experience that they catch on pretty quick with no bad habits to break, but some experience is best if you can.

The thing that you need to remember most is safety. The closet I have ever come to being hit by a bullet, which includes the ones from bad guys, over my entire career, was in this phase of training. It was a recruit that was not paying attention, and he paid dearly. This is one of the reason we train under stress. He was stressed, not paying attention to instructions, and did not clear his weapon. He fired a "negligent discharge" and missed the tip of my patrol boot by about an inch. Guns do not accidentally go off, someone has to pull the trigger. That's why we call it a negligent discharge. Someone neglected the fact that they were accountable for every round fired out of their weapon, and the safety of everyone they want to protect.

So, I have a particular concern for the safety of you and the instructors. Pay attention, pay attention, pay attention. You will get my VERY LOUD TONE on the range a lot because safety is critical. If you are unsafe, you are gone, period.

With that being said, requirements vary from state to state as well as academies. If I were you, this would be something that I would know before I arrived at the academy. This information can be given to you by the states website or your department's training officer. While I don't know every state's criteria, I do know that this is a pass or fail in any state. Know what your academy's requirements are, so you will be able to exceed them. Honestly, I cannot teach you how to shoot, in this book, without being able to evaluate your performance and make corrections, but I can offer you some good advice. If you're concerned about shooting, I would look into the following things.

Just like your body is a tool that you should have prepared ahead of time, your shooting ability should be the same. I recommend getting a coach. I have rules when I am picking a coach for shooting. First, they needed to be a law enforcement instructor, not a civilian instructor if possible. While I know several great civilian instructors, this is very different on the law enforcement side of things. I need my instructor to have a grasp on how I am expected to perform. Not to mention, you don't get to be a law enforcement instructor unless you are a sworn law enforcement officer. So there is an advantage in having someone who knows what you will be experiencing. Some of these instructors will have a range you can attend, or some will come to you.

Next, as you evaluate them, try to find one that is teaching on a regular basis. Shooting is like riding a bike, you can become rusty. Since it's my book, and I can vet this guy, I'll drop a name as an example of what to look for.

In a little town in the south Mississippi, there is a former Chief of Police named Clint McMurry. Clint is a 20 plus year veteran of law enforcement at all levels, and is an exceptional operator. He has trained and instructed at all levels of law enforcement from local to federal levels and is in peak physical condition, always. He is the owner of TruPoint Tactical, and the elite go to train with him. I know how great he is because he was my academy instructor and mentor. Not only that, he also served on the Board of Standards and Training, which is who sets the rules for the states academies.

As luck would have it, we later served on SWAT missions together, so I know his composure under pressure as well. You might not know someone like this, but that's the kind of guy I would want to teach me. What I'm saying is, find someone who understands the rigors of law enforcement training,

someone that's been where you are, and is battle-proven. Your

proactive approach will serve you well.

ACADEMICS

Just so you know, the time you spend learning is important to every instructor at the academy. We typically do not interrupt this time because knowledge really is power. Your state determines what you will be taught as a graded percentage or a pass/fail. For example, in my state, CPR is pass or fail. Report writing may be graded by a percentage score.

Here are some of the categories that most states consider by pass/fail grading:

Firearms training, defensive driver training, CPR/AED training, active shooter training, physical training, self-defense training, and several more depending on your location in the country. I know some states are pass/fail on report writing also. The criteria is set up to be easily digested. If you're having a hard time digesting, you may not have prepared properly.

Like I have already said, your mind needs to be prepared like any other part of your body. Some of you are college grads that are fresh from flexing you're learning muscles. There are also some of you that have never completed a book in your life. If you are the latter, here's a few tips to get your brain moving in a practical way.

I was a terrible student in school, so I was personally concerned about my academic ability. The first thing I did was try to ready articles that I was interested in to get my brain wheels turning again. If this is hard, listen to podcasts or audio books to get you started. It helps with the reading comprehension skills that you need. Next, I tried to find academy information online to give me an advantage. I learned some great tips, and the act of reading the materials helped as well. These little things make you stronger mentally.

It always happens, some recruits will be awesome at everything practical, but will be terrible academically. You need to understand that most of what you do in your career is report writing. It's a good idea to take some typing tests to increase your typing speed as well. All of these tips should be implemented before you show up. Work on your hand writing and memorization skills. The cadets usually have some memory work at different intervals of training. The instructors will help keep you on track.

You will be surprised at how fast you can learn when distractions are at a minimum. This is part of our symphony, and it's meant to benefit you. You will also have time to study during down time so put it to good use. Oh, by the way, I graduated with great scores in academics. I focused every second I had available to studying. Hard work typically pays dividends.

With all of that being said, the best tip that I used was asking a friend in law enforcement. Some of you are already hired and working with cops that will tell you the hard parts, academically, that affected them. If you're not hired yet, you probably know someone that is. I knew what my friend's struggle was, and a few other officers that I asked. I went the extra mile so I could exceed expectations. I say do the same thing and invest in your learning.

Here's something that you don't do. Never, and I do mean never, fall asleep in front of one of your instructors. Some of the people who are teaching you may be guest instructors that are the best in their particular field of expertise. Because I classify them as distinguished guests in my house, I will make you pay dearly in a VERY LOUD TONE and in more corrective measures than you can count. If you can't keep the eyes on your face open, then stand up and move to the back of the room, and remain standing. It is better than making the instructor think that you don't care about the material.

WHY PEOPLE FAIL THE

ACADEMY

This part is short and sweet. Through this book, a common theme developed in every category of learning. You must take action if you want to succeed here. That bares worth repeating. Take action. If you are weak in something, then care enough about yourself to make it strong. No one is going to give you anything in my house, or give you credit for something that you didn't earn. This is one of the few jobs left that probably won't be replaced by a computer. You must pay attention to ever small detail that you can think of.

So many reasons….There are bad dietary habits, poor conditioning, bad attitudes, failure in academics, failure under stress, failure in practical exams, and so many more failures that I can't count that high. It would be useless for me to try to name all of them, and anyone that can probably isn't an instructor.

We look for everything. We find everything. We will make you pay for everything wrong, because you should assume we know everything. Never replace hard work with trying to pull a "fast one" on us, we already know your game. Remember, we've been in your shoes, and some of us have taught thousands of officers since then. Work your ass off and earn it! You may never get a chance like this again, so own it!

There is one particular piece of advice I will offer you. It is the single most important piece, so much so that there is an entire chapter dedicated to it. That "piece" is mindset. It is the most powerful thing on the earth. Its why some people sit on the couch while others are at the gym. It's why some won't study and would rather be on the internet, while others have a headache from studying as hard as they can. It is the difference in all things and all places, including my house. This "piece" causes more failures than all others combined.

There are documented cases of people, most likely weak minded, that have died from non-life threatening injuries.

There is also a documented case of a Vietnam soldier being shot 21 times in the torso, and surviving. How do I know? Because I worked with him. He is now a retired deputy and one of my heroes. This is the reason for the strict mental preparedness at the academy. You will be strong when others are weak, and run to the evil rather than from it, and you will win, because losing is not in your vocabulary or accepted by anyone in my house.

WARRIOR MINDSET

I need you to read this chapter, but I need you to clear your mind first. This is the most essential information in this entire book, I'm not kidding. You will NOT make it through the academy without this! (Take a few deep breaths, and focus before you read the following)

Can you imagine what it's like, to drive scary fast, while hearing another officer screaming for help on the radio, before they go silent, only to arrive and find yourself fighting for your life in a serious gun battle, and then your gun malfunctions? Understand me now, you will die in the real world if you do not prepare your mind, period.

This is the hardest part to teach anyone, because some may not know what a warrior mindset is. A simple definition, according to Merriam-Webster, is a person who fights in battles and is known for having courage and skill. And guess what, that's what you signed up to for.

In the book "Warrior Mindset," Lt. Col. Dave Grossman says, "In the end, it's not about the 'hardware,' it's about the software. Amateurs talk about hardware or equipment, professionals talk about software or training and mental readiness." In other words, it's all about the mindset.

But what really is mindset? Is it a particular way of thinking? Is it a person's attitude or set opinions about something? Well, it's all of these things and more.

There are those that are meant to be sharpened and honed, to be the tip of the spear, with a willingness to persevere till their last breathe. A warrior doesn't need to say a word about the success of a missions that he has endured. If they survived, you know they were victorious, because they would not have left otherwise. It takes a tremendous amount of focus to prepare for battle. Most warriors are not born, they're built, and they worked their asses off for it, so I don't recommend trying to take it from them.

Former Navy Seal and author of <u>"Unleash the Warrior Within"</u> Richard Machowicz says it clearly: "Being a warrior is not about the act of fighting. It's about being so prepared to face a challenge and believing so strongly in the cause you are fighting for that you refuse to quit."

The reason you train hard, work hard, study hard, and fight hard, is because training becomes confidence. You WILL believe you can fight better, because you trained harder. You will write solid reports that make defense attorneys quiver, because you studied the laws harder. You will survive all missions, because you prepared for battle more than those who will test and try you.

This is a warrior mindset. Because I believe these things, defeating me is impossible. An instructor once asked me a question, while I was in your shoes. He said, "Do you know the difference between you and an expert and experienced martial artist?" His response was, "The martial artist had a plan before he showed up, and knows what he is going to do next."

Imagine the confidence that this instills in you. To know that you are in peak physical and mental condition, before you arrive here, or working the streets for your shift is priceless. You will sharpen this skill throughout your entire career, because that's what warriors do.

Life is not the same once you change the way you think, and it has to be this way to survive. You may go from eating dinner with your shift to a full on gun battle in the restaurant. Remember, two seconds before you got the "hot call" over the radio, everything was fine. You will go through this several times every shift. Can you imagine how mentally draining this could be without preparing yourself mentally?

Every instructor that you meet will tell you that mind and body are essential in making it through the academy successfully. To this day, I still feed my mind with knowledge that will grow my warrior spirit, and prepare my physical body to achieve whatever I may be called to do.

Another factor that we have to talk about is spirituality. I won't tell you what to believe, or who to believe in. What I will say is have your affairs in order before you go into any battle. I have prayed before every SWAT mission, every tough call while in route, and a whole bunch of other times before battle. The reason is, I want my mind clear. My training will take over because I have put in the work it takes to win, but I also have peace. I am a Christian, far from perfect, but I profess it proudly. I make things right with my Savior before any challenge or mission, so I have nothing to lose. You may kill my body in battle, but I'm going to make you work your ass off to do it, and still, you will never defeat me. I will know my purpose is complete and I have served with all I am. You may have already heard a popular prayer among officers that sounds like this: "Lord, if today is the day you call me home in the midst of battle, bloody and battered, then let me have died in a pile of my brass, fighting with all I am." The men and women that have come before you believe this as I do. It is the

difference between us and the evil we prepare you for. Being a
public servant is so much more than looking cool in your car
and a tailored uniform shirt.

If I tried to explain how it works, what the change is, it
might confuse you. It's not a thunderbolt from the sky that
makes you invincible. In fact, you may not even notice that
your warrior spirit is growing until it's called into action. Have
you ever watched an officer, soldier, or civilian hero talk about
a life changing event where they completely exceeded the level
of what others expected? Their answers are typically very
similar. Usually it is something like, "I just reacted", "I didn't
think about it, I just did it", or "my training kicked in". That's
where it comes from. That's what I'm talking about. It is
possible to be so well trained and mentally focused, that you
will act accordingly, regardless of the circumstances, without
fear stopping you.

I won't lie and say that the academy won't have scary
moments, but you will learn to fight through it, and proper

training cures a lot of doubt. To have a warrior mindset, you must be teachable. You will be able to achieve this level of confidence in your performance, if you prepare. Depending on the state you reside in, the instructors may only have you for 12 weeks and up. That's a short window to offer life-saving tools and skills. Because of this, you have to be willing to start now.

If I knew that mindset was going to be the difference in surviving, I would spend every moment available in arming myself with knowledge. It can be as simple as a motivating quote for the day or a book at bed-time. Here's a few quotes that I read often. There are hundreds more that I love, but these are some of my favorites. I like to write them on my fitness board, next to the daily workout. When I need one more rep, or need that extra push, I think about the quote. It helps me focus, and I get it done.

"Iron is full of impurities that weaken it; through forging, it becomes steel and is transformed into a razor-sharp sword. Human beings develop in the same fashion" -Morihei Ueshiba

"Training should be geared toward the motivated sociopath. Period. Those who choose to comply - will. Those who don't...will test your mettle. The truth is the training. You can't fake endurance. You can't buy confidence. You can't buy experience. When preparation meets reality, you'll get your experience. Stay safe. Train with integrity...it's your duty; it's your call." - Tony Blauer

"Somewhere out there right now someone is preparing for the day you both shall meet, how prepared will you be?" - Unknown

"Be polite. Be professional. But, have a plan to kill everyone you meet."

- Unknown

"The true warrior's greatest battle is the battle that lies within, the struggle to master the ego, to fight not for gain or glory, but to balance the scales of justice. Only when the mind is free of the concept of self can the hand strike swift and true." - Bruce Lee

"A true Warrior does not seek war, nor does he wish to do battle. He merely believes that it is honorable to cling to a worthy cause. It is noble to reach out to those who are weaker than himself and it is valiant to believe that many things are worth giving up everything for." - Phil Messina

"You can live 3 weeks without food, 3 days without water, 3 minutes without air - but you won't last 3 seconds without the will to survive." - Unknown SERE Instructor

"War is an ugly thing, but not the ugliest of things. The decayed and degraded state of moral and patriotic feeling which thinks nothing is worth war is much worse. The man who has nothing for which he is willing to fight, nothing more important than his own personal safety, is a miserable creature and has no chance of being free unless made and kept so by better men than himself." - John Stewart Mill

"We have an incredible warrior class in this country - people in law enforcement, intelligence - and I thank God every night we have them standing fast to protect us from the tremendous amount of evil that exists in the world." - Brad Thor

If you search for warrior mindset quotes on the Internet, you will find hundreds. I hope you're beginning to see the shift that is necessary, mentally and physically. Something that I say often to my cadets, and my daughter's personal favorite, is "a person is smart, but people are stupid. Watch a crowd respond to a problem and you'll see what I mean." I don't know who said it first, so I won't take credit, but it sums up the majority of what you will deal with in your career. At the end of the book, I will try to include some resources that I have found to be very valuable for promoting a strong warrior mindset.

THE INSTRUCTOR (LAST CHAPTER)

Here's a few thing that I want to share with you. First, let me say that I am no longer in a VERY LOUD TONE. It's just me and you talking like friends, seriously. If you started this book from the beginning, then you know what my VERY LOUD TONE means. I really want to connect and offer some value to this. The men and women who are instructors are people.

They all know what it's like for you to be nervous about the first day of the academy experience. They're officers first, and love what they do, but they once endured the same challenges. Somewhere in their careers, they decided that what they wanted was to help people like you, so they became instructors, which isn't an easy task. But for me, the only job that's better than being a cop is building one, so you were worth the work.

They know, through years of experience, what it takes to do this job. And, just so you know, sending someone home is one of the hardest things that I ever have to do. I have to love them more than they love themselves. I have to do what is right for you, even if you think I'm wrong. Your family deserves my best. They expect me to get you home safe and sound after every shift. What kind of instructor would I be if I allowed someone to pass that didn't deserve it? Would you want them as your partner, or covering you? Would you want them at your home, taking a report of your stolen property, when they failed report writing or crime scene processing? If you're seriously injured, and a police car can get you to the hospital quicker than an ambulance for life saving treatment, would you want the driver to be someone I passed that can't drive worth a damn?

We will ask ourselves these questions, and a thousand more, about each and every person that comes to the academy. Please understand, I owe you my very best, and will protect you with my own life if necessary. I cannot allow a man or woman to enter this profession, through my academy, that is not willing to do the same for you. This is the reason that we are the way we are. We have to lead from the front in all things that we do, for you. If I can't produce the men or women that will fight to the death to protect you and your family, then I have failed. People have the impression that we are not human, don't understand how others feel, or just don't give a damn because we thrive on the authority of being in charge. That couldn't be any further from the truth.

Some of my dearest friends are people that I've personally trained in the academy. They will tell you that my happiest day is day one. It's my favorite because I will protect you while you are in my care. I will give you all I am, to help you rebuild yourself into the perfect tool. They will also tell you, that my saddest day is when you graduate. I will hug you, shake your hand, take pictures with you and your family, and tell you how ridiculously proud I am of you. Then, after you leave, I start to think about the world that I am sending you out to. I've worked thousands of hours ahead of you on the streets, and I know what you are about to endure. This is true of every single instructor I have ever met. We worry if we'll ever see you again, and if we do, we pray that you'll be standing on two feet, and not laying in a box. This is as pure as I can tell it to you. I really hope you understand. It's all about what is best for you.

One of the things that previous recruits always talk about is that the academy seems to get easier over time. They even say that we yelled less. This is funny to me. The reason we yell less is because you screwed up less. You became a team that could band together and accomplish difficult tasks as good as anyone. The fact is my instructors and I didn't change, you did.

Here is something special that I will share with you, for the sake of transparency. It's also very personal to me, and the reason for what I do. Usually, it takes several weeks to transform a class that is selfish into those that are selfless. I watch these guys and girls go through the motions of trying to

support the other classmates. But, at some point, they really

start to care about how their teammates are doing on a very

genuine level. As I watch them grow strong together, watch

them fight together, and watch them hurt and laugh together, it

becomes clear that these tools are being honed to be the tip of

the spear. They are a band of brothers and sisters that even the

best instructors can't intimidate, shake, or stop. That's what it's

all about. That's what my house is for. We build tools here…

DEDICATIONS

My dedication is a little different than most. I am going to list the things that I'm thankful for, and give you my personal definition of what they are. So, here you go:

My Lord and Savior Jesus Christ- the truest warrior I have ever known, and I'm not ashamed to love you. Thank you for all of my missions, and bringing me home safe.

My wife- the one that tolerates all the baggage I bring home, and still loves me.

My children- the ones that give me a reason to make this world a better place, and the reason I make cadets and recruits earn it!

My family- the people that I can count on when everything seems to fall apart.

My job- the thing I'm meant to do, and I'm sure of it.

My co-workers, past and present-EVERY SINGLE HARD CHARGING, BARREL-CHESTED, FREEDOM FIGHTING, EVIL KILLING ONE OF YOU! Man, I have seen some of you do the bravest stuff, thank you, and I hope I never failed you.

Mike Walter-thanks for the ultimate sacrifice you made. Bro, I miss you every day. And, when I see those that I'm training in the academy, learning to become warriors, I hope they are half the warrior you were.

My academy class- the ones I cried with, bled with, and survived with. It started with our day one, so to you:

"BLESSED ARE THE PEACEMAKERS, FOR THEY

ARE THE SONS OF GOD"

Matthew 5:9

RESOURCES

*You can best reach me by my Facebook Page which is **Police Academy Training: Survival tips from a Veteran Academy Instructor**

*Here is a great source for motivational quotes that I use daily:

http://www.brainyquote.com/quotes/keywords/warrior.html

*These are a few really good reads:

"Warrior Mindset" by Michael Askin, Ph.D.

"Sharpening the Warrior's Edge" by Bruce Siddle

"On Combat" by Lt. Col. Dave Grossman

The is a great source for training in firearms as well as law enforcement training

www.trupointtactical.com

Made in the USA
Las Vegas, NV
23 July 2023

75150044R00042